I0020119

Python for Beginners

A Step by Step Guide to Python Programming, Data Science, and Predictive Model. A Practical Introduction to Machine Learning with Python

by

Josh Hugh Learning

Josh Hugh Learning

Disclaimer Notice:

Table of Contents

Introduction

Congratulations on the purchase of python for beginners and thank you for doing so.

The following chapters will discuss all of the things that you need to learn in order to handle Python as a coding language, and how it can work with machine learning, and a lot of other topics, making it easier for you to really work on putting both of these together. If you are brand new to Python coding, and you want to be able to learn some of the basics of Python and then want to combine it together with machine learning, then this is the guidebook for you.

The first part of this guidebook is going to focus on the Python language. This is going to head through all of the different things that you are able to do when it comes to learning the Python code. We will look at what Python is all about, how you can choose this language over some of the others, and even some of the basic parts of coding in Python that you are able to work with. We will explore how the classes and objects work, how to focus on inheritances, exceptions, conditional statements, functions, variables, and more. This will help us to gain some of the basis that we need to start coding in Python, even if you have never been able to do this before.

Once we have gotten a good handle on some of the different things that we can do with the basics of Python, it is time to move on to some of the more intermediate and even advanced things that we are able to do with our Python language, and maybe a little bit of machine learning added to the mix. We are going to look at how we can create some of our own modules, with an example of how to do this, how to do the process of multithreading, how to access our database with the use of Python, and a good look at GUI programming.

To end this guidebook, we are going to spend our time doing an introduction to machine learning and some of the amazing things that you are able to do with machine learning. The technology world is booming with the idea of machine learning and you will be able to use this along with Python to see a lot of new things show up in your coding. This section will take some time to introduce machine learning and more of what it is about.

Working with the Python language is one of the best steps that you can take to improve your coding, and even to work with some machine learning down the line if you would like. When you are ready to learn more about how to start with Python coding as a beginner, and even some of the more advanced coding techniques that will bring you into the world of machine learning, then this is the guidebook for you!

There are plenty of books on this subject on the market, thanks again for choosing this one! Every effort was made to ensure it is full of as much useful information as possible, please enjoy!

Chapter 1: The Python Language

There are a lot of different options that you are able to work with when it comes to the world of coding. Coding is not always going to be as easy as it may seem and you have a lot of options based on what you would like to do, what kind of power you want to use, and even the operating system that seems to match up with your needs the best. But one of the program's languages that many programmers like to use, for a variety of reasons but especially when they want to do things that have to do with machine learning, is Python.

Python is an object-oriented programming language that is taking the world by storm. Programmers from all over the world, and with a lot of different experience levels when it comes to programming, are working with this language because they find it easy to work with, it has a lot of power, it is one of the must use languages with machine learning and other parts of data science, and there is a large community to ensure that you are able to use it for your needs. There are a lot of benefits that come with using this kind of language for your needs and we are going to talk about a few of them now.

Python is a good language for beginners. One of the main reasons that a lot of programmers like to go with Python is because it is designed with the beginner in mind. The library is simple to use, reading through the codes is easy even if you haven't learned a single thing about doing stuff in Python, and you get the added benefit of having an object oriented coding language so you will get the code to work for your needs, even when you are just starting out. If you have ever wanted to get into the world of programming and coding, then Python is one of the best programming languages to work with.

Python can bring in a lot of power to your codes. We just spent some time talking about how the Python coding language is all about being the perfect one to use for beginners. But this doesn't mean that you are going to sacrifice computing power and strength of your codes simply because of the fact that this language was designed with beginners in mind.

In fact, a lot of people who have been working on programming for years are going to enjoy learning how to use this language as well because of the amount of power and strength that comes with it. Even as a beginner language, Python has the capabilities to handle a lot of the different things that you want to do with coding. From handling machine learning to doing data science and more, Python is definitely the language that will help you to get it all done.

Python is also going to have a large library that you are able to work with. While there are a lot of benefits that come with other coding languages, you will certainly enjoy working with Python and all that it is able to provide inside of its library. And when you need to do something like machine learning and artificial intelligence that is not found in the traditional Python library, you will be able to easily change things up and add in one of the extensions to make this work for your needs as well.

There is a large community that goes with Python. Because Python is such a well-known language, and because there is a lot of ease that comes with using this language and a lot of power, along with a lot of things that you are able to do when you choose this language a large community around the world has started to make sure you can get things done.

The program is open-sourced. This means that you won't have to worry about someone taking over the code and ruining it. It also means that the original Python is free and available to anyone who wants to download it. Of course, there are some parties that have taken parts of Python and developed them to meet certain specifications and then try to sell them. But you can always just work with the basics of the Python code without having to purchase anything else to get the program and its components to work.

There are a lot of different ways that you can benefit from this community. You will find that this community will be able to show you some of the cool things that you can do with Python, help you to progress your codes more, and even help you out when you have a question or something in your code is not working the way that you would like.

Python is going to provide you with a lot of integration features. Python can be great because it integrates what is known as the Enterprise Application Integration. This really helps with a lot of the different things you want to work on in Python including COBRA, COM, and more. It also has some powerful control capabilities, as it calls directly through Java, C++, and C. Python also has the ability to process XML and other markup languages because it can run all of the modern operating systems including Windows, Mac OS X, and Linux through the same kind of byte code.

Python provides more productivity for the programmer. The Python language has a lot of designs that are object-oriented and a lot of support libraries. Because of all these resources and how easy it is to use the program, the programmer is going to increase their productivity. This can even be used to help improve the productivity of the programmer while using languages like C#, C++, C, Perl, VB, and even Java.

This language will work on all of the operating systems. Another thing that a lot of people like about working with Python is that it helps them to create codes in any kind of operating system they want to use. You are not going to be limited based on what kind of computer you are on and what operating system you would like to use the most based on preference. You can easily visit www.python.org in order to pick out which operating system you want to use and then download the version of Python that matches up to this.

Python and machine learning are able to work together to complete some powerful codes. There are a lot of really neat things that you are able to do when you decide to work with the Python language. While you may need to add in a few extensions and libraries to get it done, you will be able to use the basics of the Python code, along with some of the stuff that we discuss in this guidebook to make those powerful codes run. If you have been working with machine learning or interested in learning how to do this, you will find that Python is the perfect language to use to make it happen.

There are a lot of things that you are going to enjoy when it comes to the Python coding language. There may be a lot of other languages out there that can help you to get things done when you are coding, but none are going to be as efficient, as easy to use, and as powerful as the Python language, and this is exactly why so many people choose to add this into their toolbelt when they want to learn a new coding language.

Installing the Python program

Another thing that we need to spend some time looking at is installing your Python program so that you can begin writing out some of the codes that are needed with this kind of language. There are some simple steps that you can take in order to get started with this kind of coding language, and it can be as easy or as difficult to work with as you choose.

Python is going to work on all of the coding languages, whether you are working with Linux, Windows, or the Apple systems. Sometimes, the Mac OS X is going to include version 2 of Python on it already, and you can certainly use this for your needs if you choose. But since most of the machine learning libraries work best with Python 3, it is usually best to go through and add the newer versions on so you can do some of that more advanced work that can come up later.

If you check your system, usually with Linux or Mac OS X (Windows has its own coding language so it will not already have a version of Python on it unless you actively went through and did it yourself), and see that there is a version of Python already on there, you will either need to work with that one, or make sure to remove it off your system so that you can upload the new one and not have two programs that are fighting against each other.

Downloading the Python language that you want to work with is going to require a few steps, but luckily, working with the option from *www.python.org* can make this easier. You can choose to work with another place to get Python, but this website includes the IDE, the files, the compiler, and all of the other parts that you need to make the system work. If you go with another website, then it is possible that you are not going to get the right version of this in place, or that you will miss out on some of the files that you need, and then you have to do extra work.

When you visit *www.python.org*, you will just pick out the version of Python that you want, and which operating system you would like to work with. With this chosen, you can then go through and follow the steps that are needed to download it on any kind of operating system that you would like to use, whether it is for Windows, Linux, or your Mac operating system. It may take a bit of time, but after a few minutes, you will find that this is set up and ready to go for you, and all of the files and parts that you want will be there.

Keep in mind with this one that we are talking about the original files that come with Python. There are going to be a lot of different libraries and extensions that you may want to use later on, such as the machine learning libraries, that are not going to be included in this download. But these are simple to use and can be a lot of fun to work with as well, as long as you already have the Python basics downloaded on your system.

www.python.org

---------------- *Example for Windows*

1. Click to Python Download

2. Click **the Windows link**, the following page will
   appear in your browser.

Python >>> Downloads >>> Windows

Python Releases for Windows

- Latest Python 3 Release - Python 3.7.4
- Latest Python 2 Release - Python 2.7.16

Stable Releases

- Python 3.7.4 - July 8, 2019

  **Note that Python 3.7.4 *cannot* be used on Windows
  XP or earlier.**

  - Download Windows help file
  - Download Windows x86-64 embeddable zip file
  - Download Windows x86-64 executable installer
  - Download Windows x86-64 web-based installer
  - Download Windows x86 embeddable zip file
  - Download Windows x86 executable installer
  - Download Windows x86 web-based installer
- Python 3.6.9 - July 2, 2019

  **Note that Python 3.6.9 *cannot* be used on Windows
  XP or earlier.**

Pre-releases

- Python 3.8.0b3 - July 29, 2019
  - Download Windows help file
  - Download Windows x86-64 embeddable zip file
  - Download Windows x86-64 executable installer
  - Download Windows x86-64 web-based installer
  - Download Windows x86 embeddable zip file
  - Download Windows x86 executable installer
  - Download Windows x86 web-based installer
- Python 3.8.0b2 - July 4, 2019
  - Download Windows help file
  - Download Windows x86-64 embeddable zip file
  - Download Windows x86-64 executable installer
  - Download Windows x86-64 web-based installer
  - Download Windows x86 embeddable zip file

3. Click on the **Download,** the following pop-up window titled **Opening python-3.74-amd64.exe** will appear.

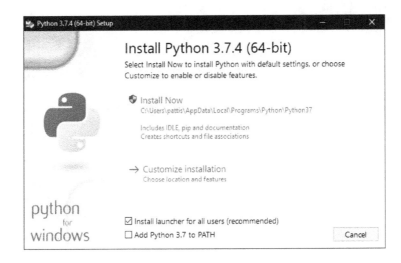

Writing your First Program

Now that we have had some time to explore what Python is all about and some of the benefits that come with it and before we move on to the different parts of the code and some other coding experiences that we can work with, we need to take some time to learn how to do a simple code in Python. This is something that a lot of different coding languages are going to work with as well and gives you a chance to explore Python a bit more, open up the compiler, and see how things are going to work inside of this language. So, let's dive in and see some of the steps that are needed to run our very own Hello, World! Program in Python.

To work with the Hello World! Program, you can open up your command line text editor. This should have come with the version of Python that you downloaded so open this up and create a new file. Inside, write out the following line:

$ nano hello.py

Once you get this text file to open up in your terminal window, you can then type out the program by writing out the following line:

```
print("Hello, World!")
```

Now that we have been able to write out some of the code, it is time to break it down into some of the different parts that come with the code. The print() function is going to be the part of the code that will tell the computer what action you would like it to perform. We know that this is a function thanks to the parenthesis that are there. This function is there in order to tell the compiler to display the information that you add into this part. By default, this is going to be the output that happens in the terminal window that is current for you.

Some of the functions, including the print function, are going to be ones that are, by default, found in the Python code. You can use them in any of the programs that you want to create and it is possible to add them in to create your very

own functions with the help of other elements that are found in the Python code.

When you are in the parentheses of this function, we wrote out the term "Hello, World!". This is going to be enclosed inside quotation marks. Any characters that we place into these quotation marks are called a string. Once we write down our program, we can exit the terminal by typing the control and the X keys, and then when you receive the prompt to save, the program will come up and you can just press y. Exiting will put you back in your shell.

Now that you have written out this program, you can run it in your program. We are going to work with the Python3 command along with the name that we gave the program file. To run the program, you can just write out the following line in your command prompt:

$ python3 hello.py

When you type this out into the command line, the terminal is going to give you the following output:

Hello, World!

Let's take a closer look over what happened in this program. Python went through and executed the line that said print("Hello, World!") by calling on the print() function like we talked about before. The string value was then passed over to the function.

For this example, your Hello, World! is known as the argument because the value is going to be passed over to a function. The quotes that we put on either side of this statement weren't printed on the screen here because they are simply there to tell Python that the function contains a string. These quotation marks are not part of the string; they are simply there to tell the compiler when the string starts and when it ends. Since the program is running, you know that you installed Python 3 properly on your system and that you wrote out the program in the right manner.

Congratulations! You have written out the Hello, World! Program in Python 3! You are now prepared to work on some of the other great programs that we will discuss in this guidebook!

Chapter 2: Data and Variables

Working on the Python code can be an exciting time. It allows you to write some strong and powerful codes that are also going to hold onto a lot of information and be easy enough for a beginner to work with. Data and variables are going to be a big part of this, and we need to take a look at how these work within our code. So, with this in mind, let's get started to see how these work together to create some of the basic codes that you need in Python.

The Keywords

As a programmer, it is a good idea to take some time to learn about the keywords that are going to show up in your code. These seem pretty simple, but if you do not put them in at all or you put them in at the wrong places, it is going to spell disaster when you are working on your code. These keywords are basically the commands that are sent over to your compiler to tell it what to do. As you can see from this, using them in the wrong manner is going to cause some issues.

If you don't put a keyword into the code, then your compiler is going to have no idea what its commands are and it won't know what to do next. If you put the keyword in the wrong place or try to use it in a different location than where it is meant to be, then it is likely that an error message is going to show up and you have to sort through the code to get things matched up again. It is best to learn what these keywords are from the beginning, and then make sure that things are in the right place so you can easily find them later.

Working with Variables

It is also important for us to take some time and look at how to work with the variables and data that come in this kind of language. These variables are basically anything in the code that is going to hold onto a changeable value. The variable is similar in idea to a box that is able to hold onto things. These are important to focus on at least a little bit because they are there to make sure that you can find them and then use a specific value that you need at a later time.

The main thing that we want to focus on when we are looking at these variables is how we are able to assign the right value over to it. To get the variable to behave the way that we want, you need to make sure that it has a value assigned to it. If the value is never assigned, then you are just making a variable that results in some empty space on the memory of your computer, and nothing is going to show up later when you try to use it. But, if you do take the time to assign a value to the variable and sometimes even more than one value to a variable, then the whole thing is going to work in the manner that you would like.

As you work with variables, you will find that there are actually three options that you can use. Each of them can be useful and it will depend on the type of code you are working on and the value that you want to assign to that particular variable. The variables that you are able to pick from will include:

- Float: this would include numbers like 3.14 and so on.

- String: this is going to be like a statement where you could write out something like "Thank you for visiting my page!" or another similar phrase.

- Whole number: this would be any of the other numbers that you would use that do not have a decimal point.

When you are working with variables in your code, you need to remember that you don't need to take the time to make a declaration to save up this spot in the memory. This is automatically going to happen once you assign a value over to the variable using the equal sign. If you want to check that this is going to happen, just look to see that you added that equal sign in, and everything is going to work.

Assigning a value over to your variable is pretty easy. Some examples of how you can do this in your code would include the following:

x = 12   #this is an example of an integer assignment

pi = 3.14   #this is an example of a floating-point assignment

customer name = John Doe   #this is an example of a string assignment

Another option that is available for the coder to work on here, and that we did mention a bit above, is that you can take two or more values and assign them over to the same variable. There are a few instances where this can be useful in the code that you are writing, so it is a nice thing to take a look at and learn how to do. It is easier than it may seem. You would simply need to go through the same kind of coding and procedure that we used above, but just make sure that the equal sign is showing up between the variable and the two values that are meant to be assigned to it.

How to Name your Identifiers

Your identifiers can be important to your code as well, and in Python, there are quite a few identifiers to work with too. You will find that they come in at a lot of different names and you may see them as functions, entities, variables, and classes. When you are naming an identifier, you can use the same information and the same rules will apply for each of them, which makes it easier for you to remember the rules.

The first rule to remember is when you name these identifiers. You have many options when you are naming your identifiers. For example, you can rely on both uppercase and lowercase letters with naming, as well as any number and the underscore symbol. You can also combine any of these together. One thing to remember here is that you can't start the name with a number and there shouldn't be any spaces between the words that you write out. So, you can't write out 3words as a name, but you can write out words3 or threewords. Make sure that you don't use one of the keywords that we discussed above or you will end up with an error.

When you pick out the identifier name, you can follow the rules above, and try to pick out a name that you can remember. Later on, when writing the code, you will need to pull it back up, and if you give it a name that is difficult to remember, you could run into problems or raise errors because things aren't showing up the way that you want. Outside of these rules, you will be fine naming the identifiers anything that you want.

The Operators

While we will take a closer look at these operators in a bit, especially the comparison operators, we are going to take a moment to look at some of the basics that come with these operators and how we are able to use them for our own benefit when writing out some codes in the Python language. They are simple to work with but add in a lot of power and capabilities to what you are doing in this language.

Operators are pretty simple parts of your code, but you should still know how they work. You will find that there are actually a few different types of them that work well. For example, the arithmetic functions are great for helping you to add, divide, subtract, and multiply different parts of the code together. There are assignment operators that will assign a specific value to your variable so that the compiler knows how to treat this. There are also comparison operators that will allow you to look at a few different pieces of code and then determine if they are similar or not and how the computer should react based on that information.

Adding in the Comments

The next thing that we need to take some time to look at is the comments that are in Python. These comments are going to be great little additions that come with the code that you are writing because they help you to leave a note or some information about what is happening in that part of the code, without having to really worry about the negative effects that come with adding it to the code. The compiler with Python is going to be set up in a manner that will ensure this is taken care of and that you can add in as many of these comments as you would like, without it having it show up in the code.

To make this work, you just need to add the # sign before you write out the comment. That sign is going to be enough to tell the compiler that you are working with a comment, and that it should just skip right over that thing, without reading it or having it interrupt the code that you are trying to write. It is that simple. You can technically add in as many of these as you would like to your code, but you should just keep it down to the things that are the most important to mention, not every little thing. This helps to make sure that the code is easier to read, that it is not too convoluted, and more.

Working with the data and some of the variables that come with the Python language can be a great way for you to get started with some of the codes that you have, but learning how to do all of these can take some time and effort to get done. When you are done with these though, you are going to be set to write out some of your own codes, and do some of the other exercises, that we are going to discuss in this guidebook.

Chapter 3: Control Flow Tools

The next thing that we can take a look at is some of the control flow tools that are available. There are a lot of different parts that you are able to add into your code to make sure that it can handle decisions, that you can deal with any errors that show up, and ensure that the program is going to work the way that you would like. Some of the different control flow tools that you can work with and can help you learn some of the basics of coding in Python include:

Comparison Operators

There are a lot of different types of operators that you are able to use based on what you would like to see happen in your code. The most common types of operators are going to be the arithmetic operators that allow you to add and subtract different parts of your code together. But the comparison operators can be an important part of the code. The comparison operators are going to make it possible to take at least two parts of the code and compare them to one another. You will have to use what is known as the Boolean expressions for this because you are going to get an answer that either says true or false. The parts of the code that you are comparing, for example, are either going to be the same, so true, or they will be different, which is false. There are a few operators that you will be able to work with that fit under the term of comparison operators which include:

- (>=): this one means to check if the left-hand operand is greater than or equal to the value of the one on the right.

- (<=): this one means to check if the value of the left-hand operand is less than or equal to the one on the right.

- (>): this one means to check whether the values of the left side are greater than the value on the right side of the code.

- (<): this one means to check whether the values of the left side are less than the values that are on the right side.

- (!=): this is the *not equal to* operator.

- (==): this one is *the equal to* operator.

The *if statements*

Conditional statements are going to be an important part of your code as well. These allow the program to make decisions, based on the conditions that you set. There are three different types of conditional statements that you are able to work with including the if statement, the if-else statement, and the elif statement. All of these are going to work in a similar manner, but it depends on how you would like the program to behave and what you want it to do.

Let's start with the if statement. This is the most basic out of the three, and it is not used as often because it missed on out a few things that you need. With this option, the user puts in an input that is either true or false based on the conditions that you set. If the answer is true, then your code will proceed. If the answer is false, then the code is going to stop because there is nothing there. An example of how this is going to work as code is to put the following code into your compiler and execute it:

```
age = int(input("Enter your age:"))

if (age <=18):

    print("You are not eligible for voting, try next election!")

print("Program ends")
```

Then we need to take a look at the if-else statements. These follow the same idea that we saw with the if statements but takes it a bit further to handle what the user puts in, no matter the answer. You can keep it simple, with one result if the answer is true and another if it is false. Or you can allow for a range of answers, with a catch-all to catch any of the answers that you didn't include. For example, if you wanted the user to pick out their favorite color, you may include five color choices in the if-else statement, and then use the catch-all, or the else part of the code, to catch any other color the user would like to use.

We will start with a basic if-else statement, going off the idea that we did in the code above. This one will catch the age of the user whether they are younger than 18 or above. The code that you can use to have this happen includes:

```
age = int(input("Enter your age:"))

if (age <=18):

    print("You are not eligible for voting, try next election!")

else

    print("Congratulations! You are eligible to vote. Check out your local polling station to find out more information!)

print("Program ends")
```

And the third option that you are able to work with will be the elif statement. These can be compared to the menu option that you would see with a game. The user will be able to choose from a specific number of options, and then the code will proceed from there. The user can not just put in what they want; they have to choose one of the options that are given for the elif statement to work the way that you want.

Let's look at an example of how this will work. We are going to make our own menu that includes options for the user to chose which type of pizza they would like to eat. You can type in the following code to help you get this done:

```
Print("Let's enjoy a Pizza! Ok, let's go inside Pizzahut!")
print("Waiter, Please select Pizza of your choice from the menu")
pizzachoice = int(input("Please enter your choice of Pizza:"))
if pizzachoice == 1:
    print('I want to enjoy a pizza napoletana')
elif pizzachoice == 2:
    print('I want to enjoy a pizza rustica')
elif pizzachoice == 3:
    print('I want to enjoy a pizza capricciosa')
```

else:

print("Sorry, I do not want any of the listed pizzas, please bring a Coca Cola for me.")

Exceptions

Exceptions are a unique thing that you are able to add into your code. These are going to either be raised as a personal exception based on how things work in your particular code, or they could be a specific exception that Python raises because the user did something that is not allowed. A good example of this is when the user tries to divide by zero, or they try to use the wrong name, or the wrong spelling, to bring out a variable or a function later on.

Knowing how to raise these exceptions can be important when you are trying to work on your code. There is a lot that goes into them, but knowing how these work can give you some more control over the codes that you are writing, and can help you learn how to anticipate when these are going to show up, while also determining how you would like to handle them.

There is a lot that you are able to do when it comes to exceptions in your code, but we are going to focus on the meat of it and look at how you can raise some of your own exceptions. The basic code that we are going to be able to work with that ensures that you are able to deal with an error that shows up while making sure that you can leave a personalized message to the user so they know what they are aware of what problem is going on so they can fix it includes:

```
x = 10

y = 0

result = 0

try:

        result = x/y

        print(result)

except ZeroDivisionError:

        print("You are trying to divide by zero.")
```

You could choose to work on the code and not add in this personalized message, but this makes it easier.

Most of the users you are going to deal with on your program are not going to be coders, and they will not understand what the long and drawn out error message is all about. With that in mind, being able to write it out and explain what is going on and how the user can fix it, like with the example above, can make things a bit easier on everyone.

The Inheritances

It is also important that we take a look at how some of these inheritances are going to work in the code that you work with. Working with an inheritance is a great way for you to have a chance to enhance a lot of the codes that can be created in Python. These inheritances are going to cut down on a lot of the time it takes to get things done while making sure that the code looks better and can run properly. Inheritances are going to be something that is new and unique to OOP languages so having them available in Python can be a nice perk.

Basically, when you decide to work with these inheritances, you will be able to take the first part of the code that you have, which we are going to call the parent code, and then move it down so you can make some changes to it, without messing with the original code that you were writing. You can do this without having anything change with the parent code while reusing and changing up the parts that you would like from the parent code.

To help us see how this kind of inheritance is going to work for us, we need to take a look at some of the code that you are going to be able to rely on when doing Python. Some example of coding that works well for this includes the following below:

```
#Example of inheritance

#base class

class Student(object):

    def__init__(self, name, rollno):

        self.name = name
```

```python
        self.rollno = rollno
#Graduate class inherits or derived from Student class
class GraduateStudent(Student):
    def__init__(self, name, rollno, graduate):
        Student__init__(self, name, rollno)
        self.graduate = graduate


def DisplayGraduateStudent(self):
        print"Student Name:", self.name)
        print("Student Rollno:", self.rollno)
        print("Study Group:", self.graduate)
#Post Graduate class inherits from Student class
class PostGraduate(Student):
    def__init__(self, name, rollno, postgrad):
        Student__init__(self, name, rollno)
        self.postgrad = postgrad
```

```
def DisplayPostGraduateStudent(self):

    print("Student Name:", self.name)

    print("Student Rollno:", self.rollno)

    print("Study Group:", self.postgrad)


#instantiate from Graduate and PostGraduate classes

    objGradStudent = GraduateStudent("Mainu", 1, "MS-Mathematics")

    objPostGradStudent = PostGraduate("Shainu", 2, "MS-CS")

    objPostGradStudent.DisplayPostGraduateStudent()
```

When you type this into your interpreter, you are going to get the results:

('Student Name:', 'Mainu')

('Student Rollno:', 1)

('Student Group:', 'MSC-Mathematics')

43

('Student Name:', 'Shainu')

('Student Rollno:', 2)

('Student Group:', 'MSC-CS')

Functions

The next part of the code that we need to take a quick look at is going to be the Python functions. These functions are simply just a set of expressions and can be called statements in some cases, and are either going to be anonymous or have a name depending on what the programmer would like. These functions are

44

going to be some of the objects that belong to the first class, which means that there aren't going to necessarily be a ton of restrictions on what you can use these for in the code.

With this said, you will find that there is a lot of diversity that comes with the functions and you are able to work with a lot of attributes to make these run. A few of the different attributes that work well with the Python functions will include:

- __doc__: This is going to return the docstring of the function that you are requesting.

- Func_default: This one is going to return a tuple of the values of your default argument.

- Func_globals: This one will return a reference that points to the dictionary holding the global variables for that function.

- Func_dict: This one is responsible for returning the namespace that will support the attributes for all your arbitrary functions.

- Func_closure: This will return to you a tuple of all the cells that hold the bindings for the free variables inside of the function.

The Loops

Loops are another important part of the code that we need to spend some time on. These are basically going to be a helpful part that cuts down on the actual number of lines of code that you need to write out at a time. If there is something in your code that you need to have repeated over again at least a few times, such as a chart or a table that you want to make, then the loop will come in and handle this for you. It saves time it makes the code look better and helps you to not have to write out as many lines of code.

There are going to be a few different types of loops that you are able to work with. The first kind is going to be the while loop. This is the one that a programmer would go with for their code when they already know how many times before they start. The code should go through and cycle with the loop. You may use this when you would like the code to count from one to ten because you know exactly when the loop needs to stop. A good example of how the code looks to make the loop show up would be the following:

```
#calculation of simple interest. Ask the user to input the principal, rate of interest, number of years.

counter = 1

while(counter <= 3):

    principal = int(input("Enter the principal amount:"))

    numberofyeras = int(input("Enter the number of years:"))

    rateofinterest = float(input("Enter the rate of interest:"))

    simpleinterest = principal * numberofyears * rateofinterest/100
```

```
print("Simple interest = %.2f" %simpleinterest)

#increase the counter by 1

counter = counter + 1

print("You have calculated simple interest for 3
time!")
```

Now that we have a good idea of how the while loop works, we need to take a look at the *for loop*. With this one, you let the loop go as many times as it needs until the input is done. This may be one time or it could be ten times. When you work with these for loops, they will not be the one who provides the code with the information to get the loop to start. Instead, this loop is going to complete an iteration in the order that you added it into the code and places it on the screen. There isn't really a need for the user to do this because the loop will just go through all of the iterations that you set up. The code example that you can use to see how this works includes:

```
# Measure some strings:
```

```
words = ['apple', 'mango', 'banana', 'orange']

for w in words:

print(w, len(w))
```

And finally, we are going to take a look at what is known as a nested loop. This one is going to work a bit differently than the other two in that it is going to have one loop that runs inside of another loop, and it is not done until both of these have reached the end. A good example of when you would want to use this kind of loop would be with a multiplication chart. You do not want to go through the code and write out one times one, and all the way up to ten times ten in order to create the code. A nested loop can take all of it down to just a few lines of code and still make the whole chart. What this would look like is the following:

```
#write a multiplication table from 1 to 10

For x in xrange(1, 11):

        For y in xrange(1, 11):

        Print '%d = %d' % (x, y, x*x)
```

When you got the output of this program, it is going to look similar to this:

1*1 = 1

1*2 = 2

1*3 = 3

1*4 = 4

All the way up to 1*10 = 10

Then, it would move on to do the table by twos such as this:

2*1 =2

2*2 = 4

And so on until you end up with 10*10 = 100 as your final spot in the sequence.

There is so much that you are able to do when you choose to write out codes in the Python language. This is definitely a language that takes some time to learn and you may have to experiment with some of the codes that come up to make sure that you are using them the proper way. But as it all comes together and you start to put some of these different parts together to form your own code, it will quickly make sense and you will be amazed at all of the things that you are able to do with the Python code.

Chapter 4: The Files

In this chapter, we are going to spend some time looking at how you can deal with the input and output of files within Python. There are a lot of different things that you are able to do with this, and you will need to be able to bring all of them out at some point or another as you are working on your code. The four things that we are going to look at is how to create a new file, how to close a file, how to look for and move a file, and how to write on a file that you have already created and saved

Creating a new file

The first option that we are going to take a look at in this chapter is how to create a new file for your needs. If you would like to make a new file that you can write out code on, then you need to open up the IDLE and then choose the mode you want to use. There are going to be three modes that work with creating a file including mode(x), write(w), and append(a).

Any time that you are looking to make some changes to the file that you have opened, you want to use the write method because this one is easiest for you to use. And if you would like to open up a file and get a new string written in that file, you would also need to work with the write method. This ensures that everything goes in the right place and the characters are going to be returned by the compiler.

You will be able to use the write() function on a regular basis because it is easy and allows the programmer to come in and make any of the changes that they want to the file. You can add in some new information, change up some of the information you have, and so on. To look at how the code is going to appear in the compiler when you are working with the write() function, use the code below:

```
#file handling operations

#writing to a new file hello.txt

f = open('hello.txt', 'w', encoding = 'utf-8')

f.write("Hello Python Developers!")

f.write("Welcome to Python World")

f.flush()

f.close()
```

In addition to being able to create and write on a file that is brand new, there may be times when you need to go through and overwrite some of the information that you have to ensure that a new statement, or a new part, shows up that wasn't there before. Python does allow for it, and the code that you need to use to make this happen will be below:

```
#file handling operations

#writing to a new file hello.txt

f = open('hello.txt', 'w', encoding = 'utf-8')

f.write("Hello Python Developers!")

f.write("Welcome to Python World")

mylist = ["Apple", "Orange", "Banana"]

#writelines() is used to write multiple lines into the file

f.write(mylist)

f.flush()

f.close()
```

The next thing that we can work on doing is binary files. This is simple to do because it is going to take the data that you have and change it over to a sound or an image file instead of a text file. You are able to go through and change up any of the text that you want to write in Python, and then move it into the sound or image. The syntax that is going to make this possible includes:

```
# write binary data to a file

# writing the file hello.dat write binary mode

F = open('hello.dat', 'wb')

# writing as byte strings

f.write(b"I am writing data in binary file!/n")

f.write(b"Let's write another list/n")

f.close()
```

Now that we have had a chance to create a file and even turn it into a binary file if it is needed, it is time to work with opening up a file to use again, after it has been closed, of course. There are times when you will want to open up the file and make some changes or work with the text in some way or another and opening up the file will help this to happen. The code that is going to make sure that you can get this done includes:

read binary data to a file

#writing the file hello.dat write append binary mode

with open("hello.dat", 'rb') as f:

    data = f.read()

    text = data.decode('utf-8'(

print(text)

The output that you would get from putting this into the system would be like the following:

Hello, world!

This is a demo using with.

This file contains three lines.

Hello, world!

This is a demo using with.

This file contains three lines.

And the final thing that we are going to look at doing here is how to seek out your file. This could help you to move your file over to a new location so it is easier to find and does the work that you need. For example, if you are working with a file and you find that things are not matching up the right way because you chose the wrong directory or spelled things in the wrong way, then you may need to work with the seek option in order to make sure that it can be fixed.

You have the ability to go through and change up where the file is located to make sure that the file ends up in the right spot, and to make it easier to bring it up and find it later on if it is needed. You just have to use the right input to tell the code where to place the file, and then make the changes to do this.

Working the files in this kind of language is going to be helpful when you are trying to get things to work out the right way in your code, when you want to make a new file, when you want to make changes, and so much more. Learning how to use some of these files and what you are able to do with all of the different parts can help you to make sure your code works in the proper manner.

Chapter 5: A Look at the Classes

One part of Python that is important and will ensure that your code is going to work the way that you would like is that it has been organized into classes. These classes are going to hold onto all of the information that you have and all of the objects and will ensure that everything stays in place and works the way that you would like. Classes and objects are going to be an important part of the Python code that is going to help make sure that all the parts that you write out are going to stay in their assigned spots, and they won't end up moving around and causing problems. With this in mind, let's take a closer look at what these classes are and even how you can create some of your own.

These classes are basically going to be containers that hold onto the objects and other parts of the code. You need to name these classes the proper way and put them in the proper spots to get them to work the right way. And you need to store the right objects in your class.

You can store anything that you want inside a class that you design, but you must ensure that things that are similar end up in the same class. The items don't have to be identical to each other, but when someone takes a look at the class that you worked on, they need to be able to see that those objects belong together and make sense to be together.

For example, you don't have to just put cars into the same class, but you could have different vehicles in the same class. You could have items that are considered food. You can even have items that are all the same color. You get some freedom when creating the classes and storing objects in those classes, but when another programmer looks at the code, they should be able to figure out what the objects inside that class are about and those objects should share something in common.

Classes are very important when it comes to writing out your code. These are going to hold onto the various objects that you write in the code and can ensure that everything is stored properly. They will also make it easier for you to call out the different parts of your code when you need them for execution.

Learning how to work with these classes are going to be super important when it comes to working in Python. These classes are going to help hold onto a lot of the different things that you need to work on in this language, will make sure that you are able to pull out the different variables and functions and will make sure that your code doesn't get thrown off and your parts don't get mixed up in the process.

How to create your own class

When you are writing out codes in Python, you have to spend some time learning how to create your own classes because it helps to keep the code organized and ensures that nothing is going to get lost. To make a class though, it is important to use the right keywords before naming the class. You are able to name the class anything that you would like, but you have to make sure that this chosen name is going to show up after the keywords are in place.

After you have taken some time to name a class, you have to go through another step in order to get the subclass named and ready to go. The subclass is the part that will go in the parenthesis. Make sure that when you are done with that first line of creating a class, that you need to have a semicolon in there. While this isn't going to ruin your code if you forget, it is considered the right programming etiquette.

Writing out a class can be pretty simple to work with but it may sound a bit complicated here so we are going to stop here for a moment and look at how you would actually be able to write out this kind of code. Then we will stop for a few minutes and look at the different parts so we can better understand what is going on at any time that we try to create a new class. The code that you will need to make this work includes:

```python
class Vehicle(object):

#constructor

def_init_(self, steering, wheels, clutch, breaks, gears):

self._steering = steering

self._wheels = wheels

self._clutch = clutch

self._breaks =breaks

self._gears  = gears

#destructor

def_del_(self):

    print("This is destructor....")


#member functions or methods

def Display_Vehicle(self):

    print('Steering:' , self._steering)

    print('Wheels:', self._wheels)

    print('Clutch:', self._clutch)
```

```
print('Breaks:', self._breaks)

print('Gears:', self._gears)

#instantiate a vehicle option

myGenericVehicle = Vehicle('Power Steering', 4, 'Super
Clutch', 'Disk Breaks', 5)

myGenericVehicle.Display_Vehicle()
```

The first part of this code is going to be the class definition. This is the part where you will take time to instantiate your object and then make sure the definition for this particular class is in place. This is important because it helps you to stick with the right kind of syntax in your code. Pay special attention to this part of the code that we have because it is the part that will tell the compiler what has to happen here.

Then we move on to the special attributes that the Python code is able to show you. These special attributes are good to use when you need to have a bit more peace of mind that the code is going to work well, and that there isn't going to be a lot of confusion that shows up. If you look through the code syntax that we used above, you should be able to see a few of these, but a few other attributes that can be useful to go along with this include:

__bases__: This is considered a tuple that contains any of the superclasses.

__module__: This is where you are going to find the name of the module and it will also hold your classes.

__name__: This will hold on to the class name.

__doc__: This is where you are going to find the reference string inside the document for your class.

__dict__: This is going to be the variable for the dict. inside the class name.

We then need to be able to assess some of the members of a class. We need to take some time to learn how to do these. You need to make sure that the compiler, along with your text editor, is going to see and then recognize the class that you could create. This is important because it helps them to execute the code in a proper manner. There are a few different methods that are going to help you to make this work when you code, and all of them are going to be good here but our option is going to be the accessor method because it is common and easy to use.

To help us see how this kind of accessor method is going to work, and to understand more of the process of accessing members of your created class better, first take a look at the code below:

```
class Cat(object)

    itsAge = None

    itsWeight = None

    itsName = None
```

#set accessor function use to assign values to the fields or member vars

```python
def setItsAge(self, itsAge):

self.itsAge = itsAge


def setItsWeight(self, itsWeight):

self.itsWeight = itsWeight


def setItsName(self, itsName):

self.itsName =itsName
```

#get accessor function use to return the values from a field

```python
def getItsAge(self):

return self.itsAge

def getItsWeight(self):
```

```
        return self.itsWeight


    def getItsName(self):

    return self.itsName

objFrisky = Cat()

objFrisky.setItsAge(5)

objFrisky.setItsWeight(10)

objFrisky.setItsName("Frisky")

print("Cats Name is:", objFrisky.getItsname())

print("Its age is:", objFrisky.getItsAge())

print("Its weight is:", objFrisky.getItsName())
```

Working with a class is not something that is supposed to be hard to work with. They can help you to take care of all the information that you have and will keep it in order so that it all makes as much sense in the process as possible. You have the ability to create any of the class types that you would like and then add in the objects that you want. Just make sure that the objects that fall into the same class are going to be similar. If someone else takes a look at that class, they understand why an object is found in that class or not.

Both the classes that you create and the objects that you decide to put into them will make a difference in the code and can ensure that it is as organized as possible, will make sure that all of the parts of your code are cleaned up and easy to read, and that they will work together well too.

Chapter 6: Creating your Own Modules

One of the things that you are able to work on when it comes to Python is creating some of your own modules in this kind of library. In this chapter, we are going to spend some time looking at the modules and explaining how the module is going to work. You will find that a module is somewhat similar to a class because it is a collection of the code of Python as well. However, the code in this kind of module is not going to be there to necessarily represent an entity. Instead, we can say that a module is going to be a collection of code that is going to work together in order to meet the same goal.

This kind of definition can seem a bit abstract when you first get started, but it is not that complicated. We have to remember that the modules in Python can contain everything that you need. It could have some functions that be done on their own, along with some classes. In some cases, there are going to be assets that are more static and different in nature including images and so on, though most of the modules that you are going to focus on are just going to be code in Python.

We are able to extend the idea that a module in Python can contain everything. We can use this to say that one module can possibly hold onto another module as well if this is what is going to fit in with the coding that you are doing. This, over time and if it is done enough, is going to result in a structure that looks like a tree. This helps us to see all of the different parts that come with it and how they are going to be connected back together.

Now we need to take a look at what a Python module is all about. As you can probably guess, there is going to be a module for Python that works for pretty much everything. In fact, there are high chances that you can probably solve any problem that is going on in your coding with the help of a module of Python that is existing. Because of this, we want to make sure that we can use the modules of Python that come from other people. This is a simple process to do, can save you a lot of time and effort, and can make coding a bit easier.

To make sure that you are able to use the module that you want in Python inside a code that you are writing, you need to work with the import and the from statements. A few things to note about this to get it to work well will include:

1. The first statement, the *from statement*, is going to be useful because it is going to help you locate the right position in the structure like a tree that comes with the module.

2. Then we move on to the import statement. This one is important because it is going to tell you which of the files of the module you would like to import. Most modules are going to contain a lot of different files, and it is likely that you are not going to need all of this, so specifying which ones you need can be helpful.

Let's say that we want to be able to work with the module that is known as Django, and we want to be able to get the loader file that comes from the template module of there. The code that we would need to use to make this happen will include:

From Django.template import loader

Now, you may find that when working with your Python code, there are going to be a few modules that are already pre-defined and that are installed with Python. However, not all of the modules that are considered Python are going to come with the original download of Python. You may have to go through the manual process of installing the code, as there are too many modules to have them all come originally with Python.

If you are working with a module that has been published officially, then installing it is going to be easy. You can use a little utility that comes with Python called a pip, and if Python is already found on your computer, it should be available on your computer already. If not, you can go through and download from the web to the get-pip.py utility that can help you to install the module that you would like. Once you have had some time to get pip set up, you can then use the install keyword and the name of any module that you would like to install. Let's say that we want to go through and install Django. We would just need to use the small code below to help us get this done.

Pip install Django

You can use the pip in a more advanced manner if you would like as well. For example, you can go through and specify the desired version, set the settings for the proxy, and so on. For most of the programmers though, this usage is going to be plenty. As soon as you have been able to install the module in this manner, it is going to have availability on your Python environment and any application that you want to use will be able to import it.

There are a number of reasons that these Python modules are going to be so popular. They are going to be there to code to scale. In fact, you can go through with a complex kind of application that deals with many problems with the help of this module simply by being able to segment the application so it comes in different and smaller chunks of code. Each chunk of the code is going to be able to help us out with a specific issue, so instead of having to handle the whole application at once, you will be able to take it in smaller applications.

This is going to be nice because it can help to make the development easier. This is because you won't have to worry about the whole picture each time. It is going to add in some more flexibility, especially if you are working with a team of multiple developers. In fact, if your team is larger enough, you can make it so that each of your developers will be able to focus on a different part of the module to get it done.

In addition, if you find that the chunks of code that you are doing are going to get too big, it is possible to take those chunks and segment them out another time into modules. This helps to make sure that any kind of application you are working on is going to be as manageable as possible. On top of all this, the modules are going to be easy to export and install any time that you would like. And the programmer can choose to publish their module in order to allow others to download and install them.

With this in mind, we are going to focus on some of the basics that come with creating modules in Python. The simplest kind of module that you are able to work on within Python is just going to be the simple file, so we are going to focus our attention on that for now. To get started, you need to be able to select a file where you would like to be able to experiment with the modules that you are doing. From this point, you can create two files in it. These files are going to be filbeB.py and fileA.py. Now we are going to start with fileA and add in a sample function to make things easier. The content and the code that we are going to use to make this happen is below:

```
Def sample_function() :

    Print("Hurray")
```

At this point in the game, we are able to import fileA over to fileB and use the sample function that we had earlier. You can write the following code that we have for fileB and then take the time to execute it to see what is going to happen here:

```
Import fileA
```

```
FileA.sample_function()
```

Since we are just using a simple function of sample_function() with what we created in fileA, we can also decide to just import that, rather than doing the whole file. To make this happen, we would just have to change up the code a bit and this would like:

```
From fileA, import sample_function
```

```
Ssample_function()
```

In both of these cases, we are going to be using the fileA module. However, we will find that this kind of module is too simple in order to scale to a real application of our choice. You are not going to be able to take this module and export it or install it anywhere you would like. And this is going to only work as long as you have both of the files stay in the same folder. If you move one or the other into a different folder, then working with this is not going to give you the results that you want. As you can imagine, this is not the best structure to use, but it gives us a good introduction to how to create one of your own modules and how you can make this work for your needs.

Working with some of the Python modules can take your coding to a new level along the way. You will find that it is one of the best ways to make sure that the work is going to show up the way that you would like, and that your coding is going to work well.

Chapter 7: The Regular Expressions

We need to take a little detour here and explore a bit what we are able to do with the regular expressions when working in the Python language. One of the things that you are going to enjoy when it comes to the larger library that is in Python is that you can work with something that is known as a regular expression, or an expression that is responsible for handling any kind of task that you would like without all of the glitches, and that are able to handle all of the different searches that you want to do with these.

You will find that working on these regular expressions are going to be good to use in Python because it helps us to go through a large variety of text, including text strings if you would like, and it is possible to use these types of regular expressions to check out the string or the text in your code to double-check whether everything is going to match up in the code in the proper manner or not.

These regular expressions can actually be nice to work with and when you would like to work on one, you can need to stick with the same kind of expression through it, even if you are going to work with another kind of coding language along with Python. Let's say that you are doing some work and you want to code with not only Python but also with other languages like C++ or Java. You would still be able to work with the regular expressions and stick with the syntax that you are familiar with when working on Python.

At this point, we have talked a bit about the regular expressions, but we need to dive in a bit deeper and get more information about it. One of the methods that you can use when it is time to explore these regular expressions is to do a search through the code for a word that you may have spelled out in different ways for your text editor. Maybe you went through and typed out blue in one part, and bleu in another part and you want to get it fixed out, the regular expressions are going to make it easier for you to see it happen.

Any time that you would like to work with some of these regular expressions, it is important to start out by going to the library with Python and then importing the expressions that they have there. You need to do this right now before we start to go much further, or it can be a challenge to do the work later on. Think about all of the different kinds of libraries and extensions that you will need at the beginning of any project and then add these in as well.

There are going to be a few different types of regular expressions that you are going to be able to use when you try to write out some of your own codes. Often, these are going to show up along with the statements, and you must be able to work with them to get the expressions to work the way that you want. To make sure that they work though, we need to spend some time looking at the background and the basics that are going to show up. So, let's get started with learning more about how these regular expressions work.

Basic Patterns

One of the things that a programmer is going to notice when they start with the expressions is that these don't just specify out the character that is fixed that you want to use in the code. In fact, it is possible to bring them out in some cases and use them to find all of the patterns that are going to show up in your code. Some of the different patterns that you need to show up in your statement, as well as in some of the other parts of a Python code, will include:

1. Ordinary characters. These are characters that will match themselves exactly. Be careful with using some of these because they do have special meanings inside of Python. The characters that you will need to watch out for include [], *, ^, $

2. The period—This is going to match any single except the new line symbol of '\n'

3. \w—This is the lowercase w that is going to match the "word" character. This can be a letter, a digit, or an underbar. Keep in mind that this is the mnemonic and that it is going to match a single word character rather than the whole word.

4. \b—This is the boundary between a non-word and a word.

5. \s—This is going to match a single white space character including the form, form, tab, return, newline, and even space. If you do \S, you are talking about any character that is not a white space.

6. ^ = start, $ = end—These are going to match to the end or the start of your string.

7. \t, \n, \r—These are going to stand for tab, newline, and return.

8. \d—This is the decimal digit for all numbers between 0 and 9. Some of the older regex utilities will not support this so be careful when using it.

9. \ --This is going to inhibit how special the character is. You use this if you are uncertain about whether the character has some special meaning or not to ensure that it is treated just like another character.

One of the ways that you are going to be able to use these regular expressions is to help you complete a query that you would like. There are other tasks, but we are going to focus on the idea of using a query to get things done. The three methods of doing a query with a regular expression that we are going to focus on are the re.findall(), re.search(), and re.match() functions. Let's take a look at what these can do and when we would be able to use these in our code.

First on the list is going to be the search method. To work with this, the syntax is going to include the function of search(). This is the one where you are able to match up things that show up at any location of the string. There aren't going to be some restrictions that you have to worry about when we work on this one, which makes it easier.

With the search method, you get the ability to check whether or not there is some kind of match that is found in the string. Sometimes, there will be a match and sometimes, there won't be based on the query that you make and what is in the code. If there are no matches in that string, then you won't get a result out of this. But if you do the query and the program comes up with a match within the string, no matter where it is found, then the result will be given back. With this one, it is only going to return the information once. There could be ten times the item is listed out, but this one will just show you that it is there, and how many times it is there. The code syntax that you are able to use with this one includes:

import re

string = 'apple, orange, mango, orange'

```
match = re.search(r'orange', string)

print(match.group(0))
```

The second thing that you can do with this is the match method. You can use this option in the same kind of code that we had before, but it is going to go through and look to see if the first word in the sequence is going to match up with your search. If the term is the first word in the sequence, then it is going to show up. If it is not, then you won't be able to get the term that you would like.

In the example above, we would be looking for the orange and seeing if we could find a match that goes with it. But since orange is not listed out as the first word in that sequence, we would not be able to get a match, even though the word orange is present. For this one to work, we need to have it match up right in the first term that is there.

The third thing that we can work with here is the findall method. If you would like to do some work and look at a string, and then get a statement to show up to release all of the possibilities for one word out of the string, then this is the type of method that you would need to use. So, if you would like to use the code above and then figure out how many times the word orange shows up, you would want to work with the findall method instead.

So to keep this one simple and to allow it to work the right way, you would just need to use the syntax that we talked about above and switch out the part with the re.search() over to re.findall(). Then you would get a new result. For this one, since we are looking at orange, we would be able to get the result of "orange, orange" in the end. This is because this method is going to be used to tell us if there are patterns or how many times that a specific word or phrase is going to show up in the code. If you had put the word in five times in the code above, then the findall method would be able to list out the word orange five times as a result.

As you can see, all three of these regular expressions are going to work in a manner that is different in order to help you work on the codes that you want to write. Each of these methods will work in order to help you find the information that you need, look to see whether there is a pattern found in the information, and can help out with so much more. Take some time practicing these to see how they are able to help you get more done in your coding.

Chapter 8: Networking

The next thing that we are going to explore when it comes to working in Python is the idea of networking. This is going to use some of the examples of modules that we talked about earlier and maybe a bit more advanced than we talked about before, but learning how to do this and the different parts that go together can make a big difference when you are creating some kinds of codes in the Python language.

Python is going to provide us with two levels of access to the network services that it has. When you look at the first one, which is known as the low level, you are able to access the basic of the socket support with the help of the operating system on the computer. This is going to be helpful because it allows the programmer to implement clients and servers whether they are working with protocols that are connection-oriented and those that do not have this connection present.

In addition to this low-level option, Python is also going to have some libraries that are considered higher in level. These are going to allow the programmer to have some access to specific application-level network protocols including HTTP and FTP low-level to name a few. In this chapter, we are going to take some of these ideas and explore some of the ways that you are working with Networking Socket Programming.

With this in mind, we need to first take a look at what the sockets are all about and why they will be so important when you work with the idea of networking in Python. Sockets are going to be the endpoints that come with a communication channel that goes bi-directionally. This means that both sides are able to send and receive messages, rather than one side or another being able to only send and the other only being able to receive. Sockets are able to communicate either within the same process, between the processes that happen on the same machine, and even between processes that happen far apart from each other, such as on different continents.

Sockets are going to be interesting and can be helpful with this networking between several processes, and even several different types of machines that you want to work with. You are also able to work with these over a few different types of channels. Some of the examples that you get with this can include UDP, TCP, and the Unix domain. The socket library that you are able to use with the help of Python is going to provide you with a few classes that are designed to handle some of the common transports, along with the generic interface that you can work with and change around in order to handle the rest of the stuff you would like to do.

The neat thing about these sockets is that they are going to have some of their own vocabularies to work with. Knowing some of these terms will make a big difference in how well you are able to work with the sockets, and what you are able to do. Some of the terms that can be helpful when you are working on these sockets and can ensure that your networking with Python will work the way that you want includes:

1. Domain: This is going to be a family of protocols that are used in order to transport the mechanism.

2. Type: The type of communication that will occur between the two endpoints, usually it is going to be SOCK_STREAM for connection-oriented protocols, and then for the connectionless protocols, you would use SOCK_DGRAM.

3. Protocol: This is often going to be zero and it is used in a manner to identify the variant of a protocol within the type and the domain that you are working with.

4. Hostname: This is going to be the identifier that you are going to use with the network interface.

Some of the things that we need to know when it comes to the hostname includes:

a. A string, which can be a hostname, an IPV6 address in a colon notation, a dotted-quad address, or a hostname depending on how it is going to be used in your code.

b. A string "broadcast" is going to tell us what address we are supposed to send the information out to.

c. A zero-length string, which is going to specify the INADDR_ANY

d. An integer, which is going to be interpreted as a binary address in host byte order.

5. Port: And we need to take a look at the term of the port. Each server is going to be set up to listen for the clients calling on at least one port,

but sometimes more. A port can be a Fixnum port number, the name of the service, or some other string that will contain the port number inside.

Now, we need to take a look at the socket module and how we are able to create one of these on our own. To create one of these sockets, we need to work with the function of socket.socket(). You will be able to find this inside the socket module, but the syntax that you are going to need to use in order to make this happen includes:

```
S = socket.socket (socket_family, socket_type, protocol = 0))
```

At this point, we need to be able to spend some time looking at the parameters and exploring some of the parameters that are going to come with this one. Some of the descriptions of the parameters that we are able to work with will include the following:

1. Socket_family. This one is going to come in as either AF_INET or _AF_UNIX.

2. Socket_type – This is going to come in with the parameters of SOCK_DGRAM or SOCK_STREAM.

3. Protocol: This one is usually going to be the parameter that is left out, and it is going to default to the 0.

Once you have been able to look through the socket object, then you need to make sure that you are using the functions that are required. These functions need to be in place to make sure that either the server or the client program is set up. The functions that you need to make sure that you are including in this kind of module is going to include some of the following for the server:

1. S.bind(): This method is going to make sure that the address, which will include the port number

pair and the hostname, over to your chosen socket.

2. S.listen(): This method is going to help us to set up and then start the listener of TCP.

3. S.accept(). This is going to passively accept the TCP client connection and will also wait until the connection arrives, which is known as blocking.

Then we have a few methods that we are able to use that are going to be considered the client socket methods. Some of the different methods that you can use that will work with the client socket methods rather than the server socket methods include:

1. S.connect()> This is going to be the method that is used in order to actively initiate the TCP server connection that we want to use.

Now that we know a bit about the different socket methods that work with both the server and the client parts of the network, it is time to take a look at a few of the general socket methods that can work with both of these. These are going to be pretty simple to work with and can work with both sides based on whether the endpoint is going to accept or send out the message. The different general socket methods that you can choose to use when doing the Python networking will include:

1. S.recv(): This is the method that is going to help receive the message of the TCP.

2. S.send(): This method is going to help to transmit the message with the TCP.

3. S.recvfrom(): This method is going to help us to receive the message of UDP.

4. S.sendto(): This method is going to help us to transmit a message that is UDP.

5. S.close: This is the method that you will use in order to close up the socket that you are working with.

6. Socket.gethostname): This is the method that is going to help return the hostname back to us.

We have spent quite a bit of time taking a look at some of the things that you can do with this kind of programming and some of the terms that you need to know along the way. With all of this in mind, it is time for us to take a look at some of the codes that we can use to make the networking behave the way that we want to in the process.

The first part we are going to look at is creating our own simple server. To help us write out our own internet servers, we have to make sure to use the socket function, which you will be able to find in the socket module, in order to create a new object of a socket. This kind of socket object is then going to be used in order to call up the other functions to ensure that it sets up the socket server in the process here.

Now, we want to be able to call up the function that is known as the bing(hostname, port) in order to tell the program which port you would like to use for the service on the given host. From there, it is time to call up the method *accept* to deal with the returned object. This method is helpful because it is going to wait until the client will be able to connect themselves to the port that is specified. Once this happens, then it is going to return a connection object, which will then be able to represent the connection that you are able to form with that other client to send messages back and forth.

This sounds like a lot, and you may be asking what you would be able to do with all of this. A good code that you can use with Python in order to create a simple server to make the networking do what you want is below:

```python
#!/usr/bin/python3          # This is server.py file
import socket

# create a socket object
serversocket = socket.socket(
          socket.AF_INET, socket.SOCK_STREAM)

# get local machine name
host = socket.gethostname()

port = 9999

# bind to the port
serversocket.bind((host, port))

# queue up to 5 requests
serversocket.listen(5)

while True:
    # establish a connection
    clientsocket,addr = serversocket.accept()

    print("Got a connection from %s" % str(addr))

    msg = 'Thank you for connecting'+ "\r\n"
```

```
clientsocket.send(msg.encode('ascii'))
clientsocket.close()
```

Now that we have been able to work with the simple server to get the network to behave the way that we want, it is time to work with the simple client. This is going to make sure that the other system is going to be able to handle the information that is coming into you and will make it work so that both parts of the system are going to be able to communicate.

We are now going to spend some time writing out a very simple program for the client, one that will make sure to open up a connection to any port that you would like (we are going to use the port known as 12345), and a given host. This is going to be simple to use because it helps us to create our own socket client with the help of the module function known as a socket.

To start with this one, we are going to use the part of the code known as intosocket.connect(hostname, port).

This is going to be useful because it helps to open up a connection that is TCP to the hostname on a port. After you have had a chance to open up the socket, you will then be able to read out from it like with any other IO object. When you are done, you need to remember to close it, just like you would be able to close up another file that you would like to use and that we talked about before.

We need to spend some time looking at an example of how to work with this code. The code that we are going to have listed out below is going to be a client that will be able to connect to our chosen port and host, and will then take the time to read any of the data that is available to it from the socket before exiting when everything is done. The code that you are going to use to make this happen includes:

```
#!/usr/bin/python3          # This is client.py file

import socket

# create a socket object
```

```
s = socket.socket(socket.AF_INET,
socket.SOCK_STREAM)

# get local machine name
host = socket.gethostname()

port = 9999

# connection to hostname on the port.
s.connect((host, port))

# Receive no more than 1024 bytes
msg = s.recv(1024)

s.close()
print (msg.decode('ascii'))
```

Now, once you are all done with this, you want to do a bit of work that can happen in the background. You will need to run the server.py that we have below us in the background, and then we can run the above client.py that we just did in order to get the results that we would like:

```
# Following would start a server in the background.
$ python server.py &

# Once the server is started, run the client as follows:
$ python client.py
```

Before we stop with this idea, we need to take a look at some of the different internet models that we may run into when we decide to do some of this. A list of some of the modules that are the most important when you are doing some internet programming or some of the Python networks are going to be listed out below.

You can look for these any time that you want to work with a networking internet module. Some of the ones that are the most common that you will see with some of your networking modules that need to be able to work online will include the following:

1. HTTP: These are going to be webpages and are port number 80.

2. NNTP: These are going to be the Usenet news and will be port number 119.

3. FTP: These are going to be the file transfers and the port number is 20.

4. SMTP: These are going to be the ones used for sending an email and will rely on port number 25.

5. POP3: These are responsible for helping fetch emails and will be port number 110.

6. IMAP4: This is another one that you can use to help with fetching email and will rely on port number 143.

7. Telnet: This is going to be the command line and will rely on port number 23.

8. Gopher. This is going to help with the transfers of the document and will rely on port number 70.

Working with networking in Python is a great way to make sure that two processes are going to be able to work together well and will ensure that you are going to see some results with communicating between the two servers or processes, whether they are on the same computer or found on opposite sides of the world from each other. This may be a more advanced method that you are able to use in order to do some coding, but when it comes to coding in Python, you can get it done quickly with some of the results that we just tried out.

Chapter 9: The Process of Multithreading

The next topic that we are going to take a look at when it comes to coding in Python is going to be known as multithreading. This is going to be a type of execution model that is going to allow us to have more than one thread at the same time, within the context of a process. This allows them to share the resources of their process, while still making sure that they can execute independently. A thread is going to be responsible for maintaining a list of information that is relevant to the execution, including the priority schedule, the stack state that is in the address space of the hosting process, a set of registers for the CPU, and the exception handlers for that thing.

Let's take a look at this a bit closer because it may not make much sense right now. Threading is going to be a useful kind of single processor system because it is going to allow the main execution thread so that when the user inputs something, you will see that it is as responsive during the process. Then there is going to be the second kind of worker thread that you are able to execute some of the tasks that are long-running and won't need to have any intervention from the user in the background to get it done.

When you do the process of threading in a system that can handle more than one processor at a time, it is going to result in a true concurrent execution of threads through more than one processor, which is going to make things faster. You have to make sure that you are able to get a system that is strong enough and has enough of the power behind it in order to get this done. If you don't, it is going to run into some trouble because it won't be able to handle both of the threads at the same time.

While the process of doing threading in a multiprocessor system is going to be faster, we have to be aware of the fact that to do this, we need to be careful with the programming. For example, we need to make sure that when we are coding, we avoid any kind of non-intuitive behaviors that show up including deadlocks and racing conditions.

Operating systems are going to be able to use this kind of threading in two main ways. The first one is going to be known as pre-emptive multithreading. This is where the context switch can be controlled with the help of the operating system. The context switching might happen at an inappropriate time. This means that a high priority thread could end up being pre-empted indirectly by one that is low in priority.

Another way that the operating system will choose to work with threading is through the process of cooperative multithreading. This is where the context switching is controlled by the thread. This is going to cause some problems, including deadlocks, if you find that a thread is blocked waiting for the resource to start being free.

The 32 and the 64-bit of Windows is going to work with the first method of multithreading, which the available processor time can be shared in a manner that all of the threads there are able to get an equal time slice, and then they can be serviced based on where they fall in line. During the switching of threads, the context of all the threads that are pre-emptied is going to be stored and then reloaded into the next thread in line. The time slice is going to end up being really short, so short that it seems like the running threads of the process are executing at the same time or one right after the other.

It is easy to confuse the idea of multithreading with multiprogramming and multitasking, which are going to be different kinds of ideas when we are working with the idea of programming and computer work. Multithreading is going to be the ability of a program or a different operating system process in order to manage its use by more than one user at a time. And it is going to manage multiple requests by the same user without having to bring out more than one copy of the program and getting them all to run on the computer.

Each user request that comes into the program or system service (and it is possible here that when it is used properly, the programmer or the user can also be using another program) is going to be kept track of as a thread that has its own identity. As the program works on its job and on behalf of the first request that comes in on that thread, and it is interrupted by other requests, the status of the work on behalf of that kind of thread is going to be kept track of until you are able to get all of the work done.

This is important because it ensures that things are able to run at the same time on the system without running into problems, or any of the work is lost in the process. Even if the first thread has to be interrupted for something more important, the process of multi-threading is going to allow us to work with holding onto the first request and lets it get back to work once the interruption is done. This is a great way to get all of the processes to get the work they want, without having to run the same program a bunch of times to get all of the work done.

Now that we have had some time to look at the basics of multithreading, it is time to take a look at this process when you are working on the Python language. Multitasking, which is a part of multithreading, is going to be the capability of performing more than one task at the same time. But when we look at it in more technical terms, multitasking is going to refer to the ability of your operating system to be able to work on two or more tasks at the same time, without issues with either one.

A good way to think about this is if you are trying to get something to download on your PC while listening to a song and playing a game or even checking your email. All of these tasks are going to be done on the same operating system at the same time. This is nothing but a form of multitasking which not just helps to save a bit of time but ensures that you are going to be able to increase your own productivity. There are two types of multitasking that you are able to do with your operating system, either process-based or thread-based. We are going to spend some more time looking at the thread-based option.

What is a thread?

A thread is basically going to be just an independent flow of execution that you are able to work with. A single process is able to work with more than one thread at a time, and then each of these threads is set up in order to handle a particular task in the program. Let's say that you are playing a game. The game, as a whole, is going to be just one process but there are going to be several different kinds of threads that are going to be able to help play the music, takes in some input from the user, running the opponent at the same time, and so on. All of these threads are going to be responsible for carrying out the variety of tasks in the same program, and at the same time, without issues.

Every process is going to be set up in a manner that has one thread always running. This one is going to be known as the main thread. This main thread is then going to be the part that can help to create the child thread objects. The child thread is also going to be the part that the main thread can initiate. We will learn in a bit how we are able to check the currently running thread to use it the way that we would like.

When can I use multithreading in Python?

The next thing that we need to take a look at is how to use the process of multithreading when we work in Python. This is going to be a process that is useful when we would like to save some time, while also seeing an improvement in the performance. But it is important to know that we are not able to apply it to everyone.

Looking back to our example of how to work with a game, the music thread is going to be set up in a way that makes it independent of the thread that takes in your input, and the input that it gets from your opponent in the game. If these were not separated out, you will be able to play the game, but it is likely that things would interrupt each other and not work. These threads need to be able to run in an independent manner. This means that you can only work with this process when the dependency between the individual threads is not there at all.

This brings us to the next point of how to achieve this type of multithreading when you work in the Python language. This can be achieved when you take some time to import your threading module. Before you import this specific module though, you need to make sure that it is installed. This is pretty easy when you work with the anaconda environment, and you would just need to use the following code in your prompt to get it done:

Conda install -c conda-forge tbb

After you have been able to go through and install this program, it is now time to import the module for threading so that you are actually able to do the process. The module for threading is simple to use, and the coding that you can use to make it happen includes:

Import threading

From threading import *

Now that you have been able to install your threading module, it is time to move ahead and do a bit of this process with the Python language. First, though, we need to learn how to create some of these threads in this language. There are three methods that you are able to use to make this happen and you have to choose the method that makes the most sense for what you want to accomplish along the way. The three main ways that you are able to create these threads in the Python language include:

1. Without going through the process of creating your own class to go along with it.

2. By extending out the Thread class that you have.

3. Without going through and extending the Thread class that you have.

Let's take a look at how each of these is going to work. The first method is that you create some of these threads without having a class present at all. It is possible to do the multithreading in Python without having to create a class at all, even though it may seem like it is best to work with a class for this. We will look later at some of the methods that you are able to use to add in a class to this, but for now, we are going to look at how to do it without this class. A good example of how you would be able to do this is below:

```
from threading import *
print(current_thread().getName())
def mt():
    print("Child Thread")
child=Thread(target=mt)
child.start()
print("Executing thread name
:",current_thread().getName())
```

Try putting this into your compiler and see what is going to happen with that code. The output is going to show us that the very first thread that we want to use is present, and this is going to be our main thread. Remember that the main thread is important because it is also going to create any of the child threads that you need, the child ones that can execute the function and then the final print statement is going to be executed out with that main thread from before.

From here, we are then able to work with the method of extending out your Thread class in order to handle some of the different things in multithreading. This one is going to be a bit different, but it is going to really help you to get things done. When you have a child class that has been created with your Tread class that has been extending, the child class is then going to be able to represent that a new thread is executing some task or another. When you choose to extend out this specific class, then it is true that the child class is set up to override just two methods ad nothing more. These two methods are going to include the run() method and the __init__() method. With this option, you are not going to be able to override any other methods.

To help you to learn how to extend the Thread class in order to create a thread, you can use the following code to help you get it done:

```python
import threading
import time
class mythread(threading.Thread):
    def run(self):
        for x in range(7):
        print("Hi from child")
a = mythread()
a.start()
a.join()
print("Bye from",current_thread().getName())
```

Take some time to put this into your compiler and figure out what the output is going to do. When you do this, you will find that it is able to show a class that the myclass is able to inherit in the Thread class and the child class. This means that the myclass is going to use the run method overriding for them. By default, the first parameter that comes with this kind of class function needs to be self, because this is going to be the pointer that goes to the current object.

Another thing to consider is that the output is going to show how our child thread is going to execute the run() method and the main thread is going to wait until the execution of the child is all the way complete. This is because the joint() function is there, which is going to tell the main thread that it has to wait its turn so that the child thread is able to finish before moving on.

This method is the one that is usually preferred when you create a thread. This is because it is seen as the standard method. But if you would like to be able to create a thread with the other method that we talked about or you can decide to create threads without extending the Thread class that you are working on and even help with inheriting. We can take a look at how to create one of these threads without having to extend out the thread class, and we can use the code below to help get this done:

```
from threading import *
class ex:
def myfunc(self): #self necessary as the first
parameter in a class func
```

```
for x in range(7):
    print("Child")
myobj=ex()
thread1=Thread(target=myobj.myfunc)
thread1.start()
thread1.join()
print("done")
```

Take some time to add this into your compiler in order to figure out what is going to happen, and to see how this kind of threading is going to happen. The child thread in this one is going to execute what is known as the myfunc, after which the main thread is able to go through and execute what is there in the last of the print statements.

With all of this discussion, it is important to take a look at some of the advantages that come with using threading. Why would a programmer want to take some time to learn how to do this, and make sure that more than one thread is going ton at the same time, rather than doing some of the traditional coding that we can show here? There are a lot of benefits that come with using this threading process including:

1. It helps us to get better utilization of any resources that we have to use.

2. It can help to simplify the code that you are writing.

3. It is going to make sure that there can be parallel and concurrent occurrences of the tasks that you have.

4. It is going to help you to reduce the amount of time consumption or response time, that is going to increase the performance at the same time.

Working with the process of multithreading or threading is going to make a big difference when it comes to the kind of programming that you are going to be able to work with. You will find that there are a lot of important codes that you want to do, and the threads will make sure that it is going to work hard on letting more than one part going on at the same time.

Use some of the codings above, and the information that we have about threading to figure out whether these are going to be the right thing to add in with your coding.

Chapter 10: The Database Access with Python

There are times when you are going to want to work with Python in order to access a database and to get through all of the information that is found inside of it. There are a lot of databases that are needed in order to make sure our information is put in the right place, that you can keep track of all the information, and so much more. Learning how to bring Python into the database, no matter what you are doing with it, can make a big difference in the results that you are able to get.

The Python standard that is used when being with a database will be Python DB-API. Most of the interfaces that are used with Python databases are going to adhere to this kind of standard so it needs to be something that you should learn about. You can always choose the database for the application that you are working on. Python Database API is going to support a lot of different database servers, which makes it easier for you to pick the one that you would like to use. Some of the options that work well for this include:

1. GadFly

2. mySQL

3. Sybase

4. Oracle

5. Interbase

6. Informix

7. Microsoft SQL Server 2000

8. PostgreSQL

9. MySQL

Keep in mind here that you need to go through and download out a separate DB API module for each of the databases that you should access. So if you need to change the API that you are working with, then you will need to list out a different module to make it work. For example, if you need to go through and work with both the MySQL database and the Oracle database, you need to download both modules for both of these.

You will find that the DB API is going to provide a minimum standard for working with database in Python and you have to work with the Python syntax and structures when it is possible. The API is going to include a few different things that can help you to get the work done including:

1. It can import the API module that you want to work with.

2. It can help to acquire a connection over to the database that you want to work with.

3. It can help to issue the statements in SQL and the stored procedures.

4. It can help to close out the connection.

Handling some of the errors

There are going to be times when your database access with Python is not going to go as well as you would hope. There are a lot of sources for these errors and knowing what they all mean can be important. Some of the different errors that can show up in this kind of work could be when you call the fetch method for a statement handle that is finished or canceled, a connection failure, an executed SQL statement that has a syntax error, and more. There are a few different types of exceptions that you can handle when doing a database, and some of the most common ones that you are most likely going to see, and their meanings, will include:

1. Warning: This one is going to be used for issues that are going to be non-fatal. It is going to be with the subclass of the StandardError.

2. Error: This is going to be the base class that comes up with most of the errors that show up in the code.

3. InterfaceError: This one is going to be used when there are some errors that show up in the module for the database, rather than in the database on its own.

4. DatabaseError: This one is going to be used when the error that you are dealing with is going to show up in the actual database.

5. DataError: This is going to be one of the subclasses that you are going to see with the DatabaseError and it is going to tell you that some of your data has an error.

6. OperationalERror: This is going to be another part of the subclass of a DatabaseError that will

refer to any of the errors that can be outside of the control of Python

and the programmer who is using it. It could include something like losing the connection with your database.

7. IntegrityError: This is going to be another subclass that can handle situations that would end up damaging the relationship integrity that shows up in the database, including the uniqueness constraints that you try to use or some of the foreign keys.

8. InternalError: This is going to be part of the DatabaseError and it is going to refer to any of the errors that happen internally in the module of the database. This could include having it so that the cursor is no longer active and useable.

9. ProgrammingError: This is going to be a part that will refer to the errors that are there, such as a bad name for the table, and some of the things

that can be safely blamed on the programmer instead of on something else in the process.

10. NotSupportedErorr: This is going to be a part that is going to show up when you want to call up some kind of functionality that is unsupported.

The scripts that you are able to write out in Python are going to help to handle some of these errors. However, before you try to use any of the exceptions that are able or try to handle any of them, make sure that the MySQLdb that you are using has the support to handle it. You can go through and read the specifications to figure out if you are able to do this or not.

Chapter 11: What Can I Do with GUI Programming?

The next topic that we are going to spend some time on is the idea of the GUI or graphical user interface. This is one of the methods that you can use for programming, and Python is going to help us to get it all done. This kind of interface is going to have a bunch of interactive components, including icons and other graphical objects that can make sure that a user can interact with any kind of computer software that you would like, including the operating system on the computer.

The GUI is a useful tool to learn about because it is considered one of the most user-friendly out of all the others, rather than using a command-line interface that is based on text, including the shell that we find with the Unix operating systems, or MS-DOS. You can think about this as the little icons on your computer. If you spend your time just clicking on icons to open up things on your computer rather than opening up a command line and typing in a code to get things done, then you are working with the GUI programming.

The GUI system was first developed by Douglas Engelbart, Alan Kay, and other researchers at Xerox PARC in 1981. Later, Apple started to introduce the Lisa computer that had this GUI in it in 1983. Let's take a look at some of the different things that we need to know when it comes to GUI programming and will be able to help understand how this is going to work better and why we need to work with this kind of interface.

To start with this, we need to take a look at how the GUI works. This is going to use a lot of different options including menus, icons, and windows in order to help you to carry out the different commands that come up. There are a lot of commands that you are able to use with this kind of interface, including moving, deleting, and opening the files. Although this kind of operating system is going to be used in most cases with a mouse, you can also work with the keyboard to make this happen with the arrow keys or some of the shortcuts on the keyboard that are there.

Let's look at an example that comes with this. If you would like to use the GUI system in order to open up a program, you would need to take the mouse pointer and move it the icon for the program that you want. And then just double click from there and the computer will know the work that you want it to do. Your program will work and can help you to open up the program and use it for your needs.

There are a lot of benefits to working with this GUI programming, especially when you are the user of a computer. Most people do not know enough about coding in order to open up the command line and get the right program to work for them. This makes it hard for them to navigate around a computer they want to use. But with GUI, this problem is going to be solved and can help anyone to use a computer, just by recognizing which icon they need to click on to get what they want out of everything on the computer.

Unlike some of the operating systems that are going to use the command line, known as CUI, which is found with the MS-DOS and Unix systems. GUI operating systems can be a lot easier to learn and a lot easier to use because you don't have to know and memorize the different commands that are available. In addition, you will be able to use this kind of system without needing to know how to use any kind of programming language at all.

This is something that a lot of computer users are going to like. The GUI is going to make it easier to use the computer, even if your use of computers and your knowledge of how to run a coding language is limited, then the GUI system is going to be the right one for you to use. Because of the ease of use that comes with this kind of system, and the appearance that is more widely accepted and modern, these systems are pretty much dominating the market for computers and coding that are out there.

Most of the modern operating systems that you want to use are going to work with the idea of GUI. Windows computers, most of the newer Apple computers, Chrome OS, and a lot of the variants of Linux will rely on this as well. And there are going to be a lot of examples that we are looking at that will work with the GUI interface including Firefox, Chrome, Internet Explorer, any of the programs with Microsoft, KDE, and GNOME.

The next question that you may have is how a user is going to be able to interact with the GUI. Most of the time, it is going to be doable with a mouse to interact with almost all of the aspects of the GUI. In some of the more modern devices, especially with mobile, it is possible to use a touchscreen to get it done. It is also possible, in some cases, to work with a keyboard, but most people are going to rely on either the mouse or the touchscreen in order to pick out what they want to do on their computer.

Users who are not familiar with GUI or GLI may want to learn a bit more about these and how they are going to work and how each is different. Even though we are used to working with the GUI because it just includes clicking on the icon on your screen and the information will open up and be ready for you to use, there are times when working with the command line can be the better option, especially based on the kind of project you want to work with. Let's take a look at some of the comparison that you can see between GUI and CLI and how you would be able to benefit from each one.

Topic	CLI	GUI
Ease of Use	Because there is going to be more memorization and the familiarity that is needed to operate and navigate on this system, many new users are going to find that it is harder to work with the CLI than it is the GUI.	Because this kind of interface is intuitive visually, many users find that it is faster and easier to work with the GUI rather than the CLI.

Control	Users are going to have a lot of control when it comes to the operating system and the file in the CLI. However, for someone who is new and hasn't used this method, it is not going to be as friendly for users.	The GUI is going to offer a lot of access to the files, the operating system, and the software features as a whole. This method is going to be seen as more user-friendly than the command line option and it is going to be used more often than the CLI.
Multitasking	Although many of the environments for command line are capable of multitasking, they are not going to offer us with the same kind of easy	GUI users are going to be able to work with a window that helps the users to toggle, manipulate, control, and view

139

	and ability in order to see more than one thing on the same screen.	through more than one program and folder at the same time.
Speed	The users of the command line will only have to rely on their keyboard in order to navigate around the interface, which gives them some faster performance in the process.	While GUIs are often efficient and fast, they are going to require the use of the mouse. This is going to be a bit slower than what we are going to see with the CLI.
Resources	For the CLI, a computer that is only going to use the command line takes less time and less of the resources of the computer compared to the	The GUI is going to take more system resources because of the elements that have been shown with loading, including the fonts and icons. Things

	GUI.	like video and mouse need to be loaded up, taking up additional resources on the system.
Scripting	A command-line interface is mostly going to require the users to already know a bunch of different commands for scripting and the syntax that comes with it. This can make it hard for a new or a novice user to create some scripts.	Creating a script with the GUI is easier thanks to some of the modern programming software. This is going to make it easier to write the scripts without having to know all of the syntax ad the commands. This software is also going to provide guides and tips for how to code some of

		the functions that you need.
Remote access	When you use CLI to access another device or computer on the same network, the user is going to be able to use this interface in order to manipulate the device and any files. You do need to know how to do all of this and which commands to use so it is harder for a beginner.	You will find that this interface makes it easier to remotely access another server or computer, and it is easy to navigate, even when you don't have a lot of experience. IT professionals like to work with GUI for some remote access that they need, including the management of user computers and servers.
Diversity	After you have	Each GUI is going

	been able to learn how to properly work with the command line, there is not much that will change with it. The new commands can be introduced to this on occasion but the original commands are going to stay the same over time.	to have a different design and a different structure when you want to perform different tasks. Even when you have an iteration of the same GUI, it is possible that there are a lot of changes with all of the versions.
Strain	The CLI is going to be pretty basic and this can be the cause of more strain on the user's vision. Using the keyboard is not that preferable to a lot of users	The use of things like shortcut keys and more frequent movement of hand positions due to switching between the mouse and the keyboard, which

	either. You have to watch your posture and pay attention to how you are using the wrists and fingers in the right manner.	can reduce the strain that comes with using it. Visual strain can still be something of a risk, but there are more colors with GUI and it is more appealing visually so this issue is not as big as it can be with the CLI.

Working with the GUI is definitely something that we are familiar with on most of the computers that we use. Unless you are planning on getting a computer that can just help you to create a program or do coding with, you will find that the GUI is going to be present on the computer. This makes life easier for a lot of users because they just have to go through and click on the icon that they want to use, and they are taken right there.

This has been done in order to cut out some of the work that is needed to reach the different parts that come with the computer and to open up the software and the applications that you have there. This may take out some of the codings that you need to do, but it does make it easier for those who don't know how to code on their own, and who don't have any experience with coding, get things done in the process.

Think about the last computer that you worked on and how it looked. When you started it up, did it have a lot of little icons for the Internet of choice, for Word, and for the other documents and programs that you wanted to use? Or did it have a command line show up and you were expected to type in some kind of code in order to open up any application on the computer? If your computer has some of the first part present, then this is a sign that you are working with the GUI, but if you see the second one, you are working with the CLI.

Both of these have some positives and negatives to work with, but knowing how they work, what you are able to do with each of them, and having a better

145

understanding of when you would want to use each of them is going to be pivotal when you are working on your own coding.

If you would like to do more with coding, rather than relying on the GUI and the graphs that are there, you may want to work with the CLI option so that you are able to write out some of the different parts that come with your own coding as well. But you can definitely work with the idea of the GUI if you find that this is easier to work with and will meet your needs in this process as well.

Chapter 12: What is Machine Learning?

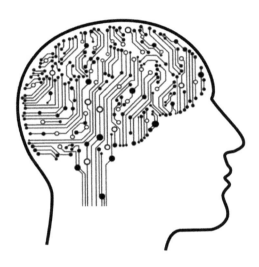

The final topic that we are going to explore in this guidebook is concerning the idea of machine learning. This is a big part of the world around us today and has changed up the world that we see when it comes to programming and coding. In fact, many of the programs that you use on a daily basis, from the search engines to look up things to voice recognition on your phone, are going to rely on machine learning and artificial intelligence to make sure that the code is able to do what the programmer would like.

It is hard for a programmer to be able to come up with all of the things that someone may lookup in a search engine or guess all of the words and phrases that someone would want to use with voice recognition or even all of the different speech patterns. Using traditional coding would make these kinds of things, and a lot of the other options out there, almost impossible. And yet, they are all a natural part of our day. And this is all possible thanks to machine learning.

Machine learning is basically a method of programming that helps the machine learn on its own. This may sound strange, but the program is set up in order to learn from the input and the responses that the user gives to any output that it uses, and then can learn how to give better results over time. This makes it easier to do some of the different processes that are so common today, even when you are not working with a traditional type of code.

There are a lot of different methods that go with machine learning, and these all are going to make sure that we are able to get the right programs done that we would like. It is also possible to add a lot of different coding languages that you are able to use as well but Python is often the one chooses because it is easy while containing all of the power that we need to make the language work the way that we want.

There are three main types of machine learning that you are going to be able to work with, and the choice you make will depend on how much work needs to go into the process you are doing, and what kind of learning makes sense for your chosen project. Each of these is found in some of the technologies that use machine learning right now, so knowing how this works and what you are able to do with it will make a big difference.

With machine learning, you are teaching the computer or the program to use its own experiences with the user in the past in order to perform better in the future. An example of this would be a program that can help with spam email filtering. There are a few methods that can work in this instance, but the easiest one would be to teach the computer how to categorize, memorize, and then identify all the emails in your inbox that you label as spam when they enter your email. Then, if some new emails come in later that match what is already on your email list, the program would be able to mark these as spam without any work on your part.

While this kind of memorization method is the easiest technique to program and work with, there are still some things that will be lacking with it. First of all, you are missing out on the inductive reasoning in the program, which needs to be there for efficient learning. As a programmer, it is much better to go through and program the computer so that it can learn how to discern the message types that come in and that are spam, rather than trying to get the program to memorize the information.

To keep this process simple, you would program your computer to scan any email that is in the spam folder or already known to be spam. From the scan, your program is going to recognize some phrases and words that appear and are common in these spam messages. The program could then scan through any new emails that you get and if an email matches up quite a bit, then it gets automatically sent to the spam folder.

This is a better method to use. But you do need to watch this one a bit. You must pay attention to what is happening during machine learning and realize that sometimes the program may get it wrong. People would be able to look at these emails and use some common sense to figure out if something is spam or not, but the program can't do this.

This can result in some normal emails going to your spam folder. The programmer would need to be able to catch the mistakes and work to show the computer program how it can avoid these issues later on in the future.

There are a lot of benefits that are going to come from implementing some machine learning in the work that you do, and you will find that it is one of the most useful processes that you are able to use in order to get things done, and to ensure the programming is going to do what you want.

Working with Python and machine learning is even better, but no matter which kind of programming language you would like to add to machine learning, machine learning is going to be able to help you in so many ways.

Machine learning can help out by taking some of the complicated tasks that you want to work with and then making them easier. Some of the tasks that you are able to explore with machine learning are going to be too complex in order to do on your own with traditional forms of coding. There may be a few of the options that you can rely on with regular coding, but they are bulky and long and hard to work with. Adding in some machine learning will make this easier and will ensure that you are going to get codes that can take on a lot of work, without as much coding language along the way.

Machine learning is going to be able to help with some of the tasks that are adaptively generated and may not work well with the changes and more that come with working with traditional coding. You will find that conventional programs can do a lot of really cool things, but there are some limitations to watch out for. One of these limitations is that these conventional programs are a little bit rigid. Once you write out the code and implement it, the codes are going to stay the same all the time. These codes will do the same thing over and over unless the programmer changes the code, but they can't learn and adapt.

There will be times when you are working on a program that you want to act in a different manner or react to an input that it receives. Working with a conventional program will not allow this to happen. But working with machine learning allows you to work with a method that teaches the program how to change.

Spam detection in your email showed a good example of how this can work.

As we are going through all of this, you may think that working with machine learning is going to be too hard to work with. You may think that it is not going to be able to provide you with the results without having to spend years learning how to work with it and learn some of the algorithms. But in reality, there are many programmers who find that working with machine learning is actually pretty easy. Sure it takes a bit longer to learn, and you need to adapt to some of the different learning algorithms based on what kind of project you are focusing on, but it can really make a difference in the kind of coding that you decide to do and can help you create some cool projects in no time.

As you work through machine learning, you will start to notice that there are a variety of algorithms that work here. These algorithms are going to handle the data that you provide to them in different manners, and the type of data, as well as the information that you would like to get off that information, will often determine which kind of algorithm you would like to use. And the type of project you would like to use will determine the algorithm as well. For example, the program you need to sort through lots of data to make good business decisions is going to be different than the algorithm that you need to make a search engine or to do speech recognition with.

Let's take a look at some of the things that you are able to do when it comes to machine learning and the different learning algorithms that you can use. First on the list is the supervised machine learning. This one is going to be similar to what we see when students are learning in the class. A teacher is going to spend time showing them a lot of examples so they know what works with that assignment and can make estimates on what isn't going to match up.

Supervised machine learning is going to work in a similar manner. It is going to rely on the idea of the programmer showing a bunch of examples during the coding process. The more samples that can be shown, the more accurate it is going to be. You don't need to show it every example that is under the sun though for a specific instance. Instead, you can spend some time showing examples out of your data set, and then, the program can be released and will be able to compare the knowledge it has to some of the input that it gets from the user. There are times when it will guess wrong and not get the result that is needed. But the longer the algorithm is able to practice and learn, the more accurate it will get.

Then there is a type of machine learning that is considered unsupervised. This one is going to work in a slightly different manner than what we saw with supervised machine learning. With this one, you will not need to spend time showing a lot of examples to the computer in order to get the results that you want. You can let the program learn on its own, based on the feedback it is getting from the outputs it provides.

A good example of this is a search engine. There is no way that the programmer is going to be able to come in and think about all the search terms and the best results that go with it. This can make it impossible to work with supervised machine learning algorithms. But the unsupervised machine learning is going to be able to do this because it can search for the results that it needs, and then, depending on the results that it gets from the user, it is going to be able to make adjustments and get better.

To start, we should look at how the search engine works. The first time that you use a new search engine, the results are not always going to provide you with what you want at the top of the results. But as you make your selections, the search engine will make adjustments and it will start to give you the right results that will match up with what you want.

And then there is reinforcement machine learning. This is going to be similar to what we are able to see with the unsupervised machine learning, but it is going to focus more on the idea of true or false. The program is going to learn based on whether the output they use is true, or if it is false, to the user, and then make the right adjustments that are needed to ensure that it learns and starts to give off the right answers that are needed.

As you can see, there is a lot that you are able to do when it comes to machine learning, and using the Python language is going to make it easier to really make this work for your needs. And with a lot of the future programming that we are going to learn how to do, and even some of the different projects that may seem the best for you later on and now, you will find that machine learning is going to be an important topic to work with. If you are particularly interested in this topic, you can find more detailed information in my book *Python Machine Learning*.

Conclusion

Thank you for making it through to the end of *Python for Beginners.* Let's hope it was informative and able to provide you with all of the tools you need to achieve your goals whatever they may be.

The next step is to start practicing some of the codings that we spent time in this guidebook. We spent a lot of time exploring the different things that you are able to do with Python and a lot of the different aspects that are going to show up in your own coding adventures. While we may not have gone into as much depth as you would see in other locations, we made sure that we knew what each part was about and explored the actual coding that you would need to do with this.

Many people are scared to get into any type of coding because they think that it will be too hard or that they will never be able to figure it all out. But when they take a look at Python, they see how easy coding can be. That is what this guidebook took some time to look at this, and looked at some of the different codes that you want to write with this kind of coding language. We also took it a bit of the more advanced types of coding that you can do with this language as well, ensuring that you are going to be able to get the results that you would like.

There are a lot of things that you are able to do with the Python language and how you can use it with machine learning. This guidebook is going to take some time to look at all of these aspects so you can do some of the codings in the process. When you are ready to begin your journey with Python, make sure to check out this guidebook to help you get started!

If you found this book useful in any way, a review on Amazon is always appreciated !

Josh Hugh Learning

www.ingramcontent.com/pod-product-compliance
Lightning Source LLC
Chambersburg PA
CBHW071130050326
40690CB00008B/1413